"The Sports Backers is proud to be the Richmond region's advocate of sports and sports tourism. Backed by our corporate champions and thousands of community volunteers, we strive to strengthen the area's economy and quality of life through events such as the Ukrop's Monument Avenue 10k and Dominion Riverrock. These programs, along with the many others that you will read about in this book, have helped position Richmond as a haven for sports enthusiasts. While excited by tales from Richmond's legendary sports past, we are even more excited to create new storylines during the next century."

Co-Authors

Brooks Smith & Wayne Dementi

Foreword By
Jerry Lindquist

© Copyright 2010
by Dementi Milestone Publishing
1530 Oak Grove Drive
Manakin-Sabot, VA 23103

ISBN: 978-0-9827019-2-8

Brooks Smith & Wayne Dementi
Co-Authors

For information write:

Dementi Milestone Publishing
1530 Oak Grove Drive
Manakin-Sabot, VA 23103
www.dementimilestonepublishing.com

Jayne Hushen, Graphic Design
www.HushenDesign.com

Cover photo: University of Richmond football from U of R yearbook, circa 1930.

Sports in Richmond

Foreword

So, what do you think: Is Richmond a great sports town? Or not?

The debate rages, usually after the latest – and greatest – professional franchise goes belly-up or takes the long road south.

We certainly suffered our share of lost opportunities during the six decades (or parts thereof) that I was paid to watch kids' games by the *Richmond Times-Dispatch*. Just consider hockey's Robins, Wildcats (lived and died in fewer than six months), Rifles, Renegades I, RiverDogs, and Renegades II; baseball's Virginians and Braves; semi-pro football's Rebels, Mustangs, and Road Runners; indoor football's Bandits and Speed; and a handful of basketball teams (men's and women's), the names of which only the most diehard fans will recall.

Professional tennis once was a recurring annual attraction until it became too costly to sustain. We hosted National Football League preseason games – Redskins, George Halas-led Chicago Bears, and the New York Jets with Joe Willie Namath – at City Stadium. The NCAA liked the Coliseum just long enough to give Richmond a women's national hoops final and men's regionals before moving on.

So, what's the problem? Are we not worthy?

With rare exception (think Kickers and NASCAR), we have perennial problems maintaining interest at the box office. But that doesn't make us un-worthy. To the contrary, Richmond is a great sports town because we're bright enough to recognize good from bad and will stop paying to watch the latter; and, frankly, we'd rather take an active role in something than sit on our hands and settle for being just spectators.

Golf, tennis, and softball know no bounds here. Competitive swimming and little league baseball flourish in record numbers among our youth. And many of our kid-athletes have gone on to become stars on a larger stage.

Beyond the professional franchise, Richmond has a rich sports heritage for which all of us can be proud. In the pages that follow, Brooks Smith and Wayne Dementi bring you many of the sights and sounds of a great sports town. Settle back and enjoy.

Jerry Lindquist went to work for the <u>Richmond Times-Dispatch</u> two weeks after graduating from Washington and Lee in 1949. He stayed for 47 years. The great sports editor, Chauncey Durden, once quipped that he thought he was only hiring Jerry for the summer. Talk about "the longest summer!" Jerry was inducted into the Virginia Sports Hall of Fame (media wing) in 2003.

Dedication

This book is dedicated to the home run,
the eagle, the ace; to the games we won,
the games we lost, and above all else,
the games we played.

Brooks Smith
and
Wayne Dementi

About the Authors

Brooks Smith is a lawyer by profession and a writer by heart. His essays, which have aired regularly on WCVE Public Radio since 2005, celebrate the nearly forgotten storylines of Richmond.

Whether on air or in print, Brooks' writing is whimsical, irregular, and perhaps even prose-like. Wayne Farrar, WCVE Public Radio's News Director, once described Brooks as having "the tenacity of a historian, the curiosity of a journalist, and the soul of a poet."

If any of this is true, then Brooks ascribes it to the soulful city he calls home, where stories seem to accrete on the banks of the James like so many pieces of driftwood. Brooks practices environmental law at Hunton & Williams LLP, and lives in Richmond with his wife, Jennifer, and three children, Emma, Ethan, and Christian.

Wayne Dementi is a photographer, past president of Dementi Studio, and member of a family of photographers that has been capturing Richmond's most iconic landmarks and people for nearly a century. Wayne released his first book, *Celebrate Richmond*, in the fall of 1999. The book quickly became a best seller, and inspired Wayne to author or collaborate on over 25 other books in the past decade.

Wayne is as accomplished at storytelling as he is at camera work, and his tales of old and forgotten Richmond have delighted audiences far and near. Wayne lives in rural Goochland County with his wife, Dianne. Their grown children adventure around Richmond just like Wayne did as a child, driving ever so slowly with his dad to capture that perfect streak of light, or air, or cover of cloud.

Brooks and Wayne also co-authored *Facts and Legends of the Hills of Richmond*, which was released in 2008, and *Songlines of Richmond*, which was released in 2009.

Introduction

Richmond's sporting tradition is old, nearly mythical. We lay claim to the oldest recorded game of cricket in the New World; the fastest racehorse; one of the most famous quoit clubs in the country; the first forward pass in college football; and all manner of strange games inspired by the river, the strangest of which may be lassoing and riding sturgeon, those primordial giants of the James.

Our sporting tradition is also rich in heroes. We are home to Arthur Ashe, the great sportsman, humanitarian, and historian; Ray Dandridge, the finest third baseman never to play major league baseball; Tuckahoe Little League, which launched a group of 12-year olds to international fame in 1968; Olympians like Harold Thompson Mann, who became the first person to swim the 100-meter backstroke in less than a minute; and modern superstars like Johnny Newman and Justin Verlander, whose legacies continue to unfold.

Of course, all sports can be reduced to moments in time.

Moments *suspended* in time. Moments of greatness, of disbelief, of the immense potential of the human body and spirit. In 1949, Slammin' Sammy Snead came from behind five times to win the PGA Championship,

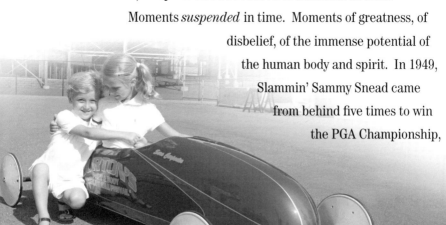

the only golf major to be played on Virginia soil. In 1963, Ned Jarrett traded leads with Richard Petty four times before Jarrett's Ford beat out Petty's Plymouth for a NASCAR Grand National victory at Southside Speedway, the toughest short track in the South. In 1968, the New York Jets played their season opener against Joe Namath and the Boston Patriots at City Stadium. In 1970, Billie Jean King broke rank from the tennis establishment and won the first of the Virginia Slims Invitational series at Westwood. And in 1996, Lance Armstrong endured four grueling climbs up Taylor's Hill to win the Tour DuPont.

Our sporting tradition prospers. Rowing has returned to the James, renewing a tradition that dates back to 1876. Tens of thousands of children have been introduced to soccer. At least as many more play tennis, baseball, football, and basketball. Each spring, nearly 40,000 runners descend on the streets of Richmond for the Ukrop's Monument Avenue 10k. Each summer, a new generation of racers takes the hill for the soap box derby. And each fall, more than 15,000 runners participate in the races of the Richmond Marathon, including six fabled "Old Lions" who have run each and every marathon since 1978.

Some lament the absence of a big league team, or a big league stadium, in our fair city. But our sporting tradition is less about watching than doing. We play sports. From rank amateur to elite athlete, we inspire and sustain more players than most big league cities. And by the look of it, we have more fun than they do, too.

TIME

This timeline reflects some of our favorite moments in Richmond an adventure map, it hints at what lays in between.

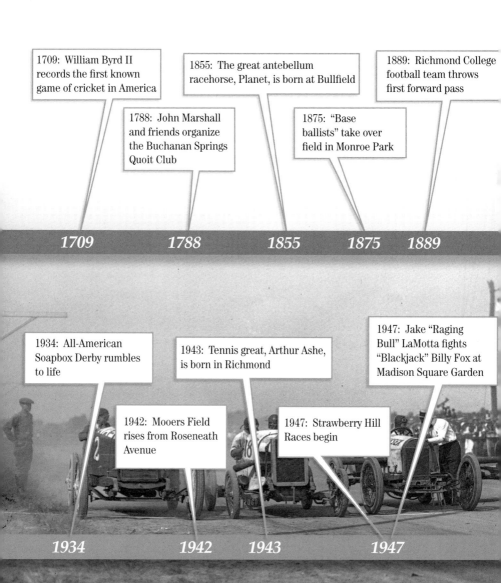

1709: William Byrd II records the first known game of cricket in America

1788: John Marshall and friends organize the Buchanan Springs Quoit Club

1855: The great antebellum racehorse, Planet, is born at Bullfield

1875: "Base ballists" take over field in Monroe Park

1889: Richmond College football team throws first forward pass

1709   **1788**   **1855**   **1875**   **1889**

1934: All-American Soapbox Derby rumbles to life

1942: Mooers Field rises from Roseneath Avenue

1943: Tennis great, Arthur Ashe, is born in Richmond

1947: Strawberry Hill Races begin

1947: Jake "Raging Bull" LaMotta fights "Blackjack" Billy Fox at Madison Square Garden

1934   **1942**   **1943**   **1947**

L I N E

sports over the centuries. It is by no means complete, but like

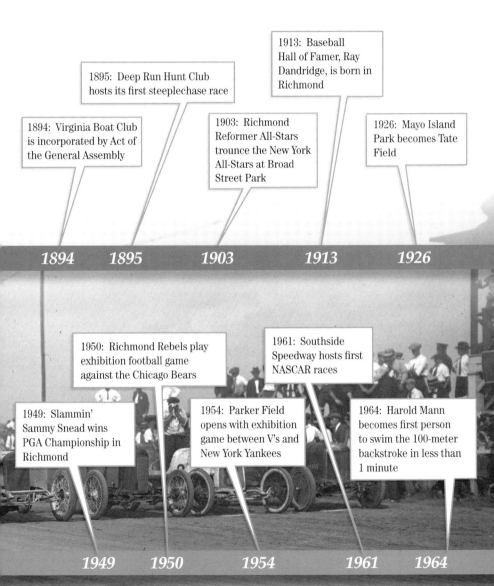

1894: Virginia Boat Club is incorporated by Act of the General Assembly

1895: Deep Run Hunt Club hosts its first steeplechase race

1903: Richmond Reformer All-Stars trounce the New York All-Stars at Broad Street Park

1913: Baseball Hall of Famer, Ray Dandridge, is born in Richmond

1926: Mayo Island Park becomes Tate Field

1894 **1895** **1903** **1913** **1926**

1949: Slammin' Sammy Snead wins PGA Championship in Richmond

1950: Richmond Rebels play exhibition football game against the Chicago Bears

1954: Parker Field opens with exhibition game between V's and New York Yankees

1961: Southside Speedway hosts first NASCAR races

1964: Harold Mann becomes first person to swim the 100-meter backstroke in less than 1 minute

1949 **1950** **1954** **1961** **1964**

1964: TJ High School becomes first and only public school with a soccer team

1968: Jets and Patriots play season opener at City Stadium

1978: The Old Lions run their first Richmond marathon

1968: Tuckahoe Little League marches to national title and Little League World Series

1970: Virginia Slims women's tennis tournament series kicks off at Westwood Club

1964   1968   1970   1978

1985: The Diamond is named in honor of regional cooperation

1989: Tour de Trump debuts with bicycle race through Richmond

1984: Johnny Newman helps propel UR basketball team to NCAA tourney

1988: Richmond hosts first of three consecutive Bass Masters Classics, the Super Bowl of fishing

1984   **1985**   **1988**   **1989**

The Boys of Summer:
1968 Tuckahoe Little League

If you tell a friend that he peaked at the age of 12, he may take it as an insult. But if you tell that to a player from the 1968 Tuckahoe Little League Team, well, he'll smile a smile a mile wide and, if you're lucky, he'll spin you a story that beats any sports story in our fair city, hands down.

In 1968, our Tuckahoe Little League team became champions of the United States and fell just one run short of becoming champions of the world. That run may persist as a tooth in the jaws of defeat, but for our boys of summer, it is just a blue note in a riff that rivals the best of our jazz greats.

On July 1, 1968, 27 boys were selected from little league teams around the city to try out for an all-star team. The roster was winnowed down to 14 players and two alternates under the helm of skipper Wesley Voltz and his assistant Harry Humphrey. After a scant two weeks of practice, the team was thrown into single elimination play – first local, then regional, and then beyond. In the first 11 games, the team

Roger Miller, Tuckahoe Little League player, shown with an opponent from Japan at Williamsport, 1968.

1

Johnny Mizelle and Roger Miller.

blistered its opponents with nine shut-outs, some as one-sided as 17-0 (against Varina) and 18-0 (against Gordonsville). Wending their way through the south, our little league all-stars beat St. Albans, West Virginia 3-0, Valley Sports, Kentucky 3-2, Lubbock, Texas 10-0, and Donelson, Tennessee 3-0. They went from the district championships to the state, the southern regional, and then, at last, to the Little League World Series in Williamsport, Pennsylvania.

Just one month into its existence as a team, Tuckahoe beat Terre Haute in the quarterfinals 6-2, and Quebec in the semis 8-5. By the time of the finals against Osaka, Japan, our team was "big-time." More than 25,000 fans packed into the ballpark to watch the game, and

Little League International Complex in Williamsport, Pennsylvania, taken at Little League World Series, 1968.

millions more followed it on *ABC's Wide World of Sports*. Though the final score showed our boys down 1-0, no score could tell the full measure of their triumphs. Roger Miller threw nine no-hitters over the course of the season, five in the tournament alone. Hank Stoneburner threw another two. John Mizelle sustained the team's streak with an amazing, come-from-behind, rain-delayed win in West Virginia, and Gray Oliver added fireworks of his own. Truly every player on the team was MVP at one moment or another, which is why they were known for their collective scrap, skill, and nearly perfect timing.

Jim Pankovits, Roger Miller and Hank Stoneburner.

On the way back, the boys stopped at the White House for a tour hosted by Vice President Hubert Humphrey. Richmonders welcomed them home with a ticker tape parade down Broad, then visits with the governor, congressmen, senators, and other visiting dignitaries. And before the day was down, our team took the bases with the Richmond Braves at Parker Field as part of a special fan appreciation event.

Tuckahoe Little League remains vibrant today. Building on more than 50 years of excellence, it continues to demonstrate its commitment to sportsmanship, teamwork, courage, and hard work through world class runs in 1968, 1976, and 1993, as well as exceptional athletes like Jim Pankovits from the storied '68 team and Justin Verlander of more recent fame. These days, we may be consumed by big league play and big league players, but in my humble opinion, the soul of baseball survives in the experience of little leaguers, and 12-year-olds, and jazz anthems like this one from 1968.

The Curious Game of Quoits

Have you ever driven down Monument Avenue on a pretty spring day and witnessed hoards of happy kids tossing beanbag sacks into makeshift "bag-o" boxes? Well, flash back a few hundred years and you may just as well have seen some of our most famous founding fathers tossing quoits. The game as it was back then involved a circular disk with a hole in the middle called a quoit, and a metal stake in the ground called a hob or a meg. Players would stand at a distance of 20 feet or so from the hob, and then try to toss the quoit as close as they could. You can imagine the cheers of the day – "ring the meg" or "miss the meg" – depending on your affinity for the player with quoits in hand.

◀ *Quoit pit in the backyard of the John Marshall House. Richmond, Virginia.*

The game of quoits is considered to be ancient in origin, but it has been almost fully eclipsed by horseshoes in more modern times. As the rumor goes, horseshoes were simply easier to find by soldiers tracking horses during the Civil War. And ringers – the imperturbable crowd favorite – proved easier to toss with open shoes than closed disks.

But quoits are a game of pedigree, particularly here in Richmond. One of the oldest and most famous quoit clubs in the country started here in 1788, right around the epicenter of what is now VCU's campus at 1000 West Broad Street. The club operated out of Parson Buchanan's farm, which was equally famous for its idyllic, oak grove setting as for its origins in William Byrd III's land lottery. Reciting the club roster is like listing a who's who in early American politics. Prominent among the membership were Chief Justice John Marshall, U.S. Attorney General William Wirt, U.S. Senator Watkins Leigh, and defense lawyer John Wickham. Marshall was reported to be a fierce competitor and a keen judge – not just of the treasons of the day, but also over all disputes involving closest quoit to the meg.

The old Buchanan Springs Quoit Club would meet regularly on Saturdays between May and October. Club members would eat prodigious amounts of food and drink to abandon out of a big bowl of rum punch, julep, or toddies. Thus sated, they would take to the field with quoits in hand. You could expect an equal measure of playing, storytelling, and plain tomfoolery, but by club rules, any discussion of politics was strictly prohibited.

The Virginia Historical Society has among its archives an invitation, addressed to Governor Wise, to join in the festivities of the Buchanan Springs Quoit Club as an honorary member on July 12, 1856. Imagine the delight of the Governor and others to read an invitation to quoits that begins like this: "It is made my duty and I will add my pleasure to inform you..."

Alas, quoits are long gone, and the feasts in the old oak grove are just a memory. But try telling this to those hoards of happy kids on Monument and they'll probably hand you a beanbag sack and invite you to join in their festivities. The invitation might be different than it was back in the day, but the games, and the storytelling, and the plain tomfoolery are probably about the same.

QUOITS.

Richmond College Football and the First Forward Pass

Richmond College formed its first club football team in 1878, less than a decade after the first intercollegiate game in America. Though modern football tends to be characterized by less brain than brawn, our Richmond College team was formed by two decidedly brainy literary societies.

The rules of the day were considerably different than now. Back then, up to 40 players took the field for any given play. A first down required a gain of only five yards, but you only had three tries to get one. The field itself was 110 yards long. Players did not wear helmets, and passing was illegal. On most plays, the team with the ball would simply form a giant wedge and try to grind the ball forward. According to Richmond's football historian *emeritus*, John Wendell Bailey, quarterbacks were strategically small and occasionally equipped with straps on their pants so that linesmen could pick them up and heave them over the line of scrimmage.

The University of Richmond wins the FBS National Championship. Chattanooga, Tennessee, 2008.

9

The "holy grail" for many football aficionados is pinpointing the exact moment of the first forward pass. By intercollegiate rules, the pass was not even legal until 1906, and most historians mark the first illegal pass just a few years earlier. But with thanks to Professor Bailey for recording our early roots, Richmond might be able to

claim this storied prize. According to a newspaper account of an intercollegiate game played between Richmond College and Randolph-Macon College in 1889, Richmond dominated with repeated forward

UR Quarterback Buster O'Brien receives the MVP trophy following the Spiders' win over Ohio at the Tangerine Bowl, 1969.

Richmond Spiders, 1917.

passes, including one for a 50-yard touchdown in the second half.

Richmond can also claim some amazing football statistics. In 1881, Richmond went 2 and 0 for its first perfect season. In 1882, Richmond repeated perfection by going 1 and 0. Alas, in 1883, the only scheduled game was rained out, giving new meaning to the old sports adage, *"sometimes you win, sometimes you lose, and sometimes it rains."* Richmond's most lopsided win was 80-0 against Randolph-Macon in 1917. Its most lopsided loss was 0-84 against Georgetown in 1900. And in 1911, Richmond went the entire season without scoring a single point, earning the nickname, *Scoreless Wonders*. Happily, Richmond's stunning successes in recent years obscure this nickname from the past.

Opening Day, E. Claiborne Robins Stadium. September 18, 2010. The UR Spiders defeat Elon 27-21 in overtime.

PLANET

VIRGINIA'S UNRIVALLED
RACE HORSE

This renowned Racer and Stallion will make his season of 1866, at **BULLFIELD**, the farm of Major **THOMAS DOSWELL**, in the county of **HANOVER**, twenty-four miles above Richmond, commencing March 1st, and ending July 15th, at $50 the season, with $2 to the groom.

Special attention will be given to the care and management of Mares sent to him, but in no event will be responsible for accidents.

They shall be fed with grain at 50 cents per diem.

All charges must be paid before the Mares are taken away.

THOMAS & THOMAS W. DOSWELL.

Planet: The Fastest Racehorse in the South

Back in 1783, a German visitor remarked that Richmond was like an Arabian village teeming with horses at every turn. And we've been a horse-crazy kind of place ever since.

Without question, our most famous race horse was Secretariat, a triple crown winner who still holds speed records at the Kentucky Derby and the Belmont Stakes. Secretariat was born just up the road in Doswell in 1970.

Major Thomas Doswell

Secretariat's larger-than-life mystique tends to eclipse the triumphs of his stable mate, Riva Ridge, who won two legs of the triple crown in 1972, just a year before Secretariat took all three. And if Riva Ridge pales by comparison, then so too the many fine thoroughbreds who raced on Virginia turf over the centuries. Among these forerunners (pun intended), one deserves special mention.

Planet was born in 1855 at an old, nearly forgotten farm called Bullfield along the Pamunkey River in Hanover County. The "great red fox," as he was known, was owned by Major Thomas Doswell, for whom the Town of Doswell is named. In the years leading up to the American Civil War, Planet won 27 out of 31 races at tracks all around the country, from Ashland to New Orleans, and Savannah to New

Part of the stables at Bullfield, Hanover, Co.,

owing the stall where Planet was foaled.

York. In each of the four races Planet lost, he came in a close second. Planet's record is even more remarkable when viewed by the lengths he went to win. Many of Planet's races were 4 miles long (compared to the 1 to 1 ½ mile races of more modern times), and he sometimes ran as many as 12 miles in a single afternoon.

With thanks to some loyal local horse lovers, Planet is now a candidate for induction into the Thoroughbred Racing Hall of Fame in Saratoga Springs, New York. And with continued focus on our great turf tradition, Richmond may one day return to the "golden age of horse racing" that marked Planet's remarkable run.

Slammin' Sammy: 1949 PGA Championship

The only golf "major" to be played on Virginia soil took place more than a half-century ago right here in Richmond at the old Hermitage Club, now known as Belmont. The year was 1949 and the "major" was the PGA Championship, considered at the time to be "the greatest sports event in the history of Father Byrd's town." In addition to an A-list of professional golfers, the event attracted the top sports writers in the country, including O.B. Keeler of the *Atlanta Journal*, who was considered to be the dean of golf writers.

The winner was Slammin' Sammy Snead, a Virginia native and the unequivocal "people's choice." Snead turned 37 during the tournament, becoming the oldest player at the time to win a PGA Championship and the first to win both the Masters and PGA in the same year. A week after his win in Richmond, Snead competed in the U.S. Open, but ended up in second place, just a stroke away from sweeping the "triple crown" of golf's majors.

Of course, no golf story is complete without a few tall tales. The first involves Jack Burke, who was Snead's match play competitor

1949 PGA Winner Sam Snead shown with Margaret Galloway Ford, Sheila Robertson Ford, and "Butch."

Sam Snead, coming out of the rough at Hermitage Country Club, during the PGA Championship, 1949.

17

Belmont Recreation Center and Golf Course, 2010.

in round one of the tournament. Burke lost his caddy, a first-timer on the course, who strayed from the 13th green to the 16th tee and remained happily lost until a jeep was dispatched to retrieve him. Burke quipped after the round that he'd lost enough holes to Snead without having to lose his caddy too. The second involves Snead's winning putter, which reportedly was borrowed from a boy Snead met earlier in the year. In the locker room after his victory in Richmond, Snead was pressed for the boy's name, but he wouldn't say for fear that the boy would ask for his putter back.

The PGA Championship is considered to be the "most grueling test in all golfdom," and Snead surely bore this out in his five come-from-behind wins during the '49 tournament. For his efforts, Snead won a whopping $3,500. Amazingly, this put him at the top of the money leader board with $12,610.83 for the year (including previous wins at the Greensboro Open and Masters).

Golf has surely changed over the years, with staggering purses, rock star egos, razor thin fairways, and greens so finely manicured that only a rare few have the opportunity to play. But here in Richmond, the legacy of our last major persists. And the course on which it was played, a course described as "not rugged but sly," remains open to all – young and old, high handicap and low – for just shy of $25 a round. So if you're looking to spoil a good walk, or lose a few golf balls, why not see if you can out-putt Slammin' Sammy just down the road at Belmont. I may even have a putter for you to borrow.

Soap Box Heroes

The All-American Soap Box Derby rumbled to life way back in
1934 through one of those happy accidents that seem to accompany
the mother of all great inventions. As the story goes, a photographer
for a Dayton, Ohio paper happened to come across three boys racing
home-made go-carts down the street. The photographer, a fellow
named Myron Scott, was known for creative thinking, and somewhere
in the recesses of his mind's eye, he captured not only the iconic
image of boys behaving like boys, but also the idea for a grand-scale
national youth racing competition.

More than a million racers later, Scott's vision has become what is
affectionately and perhaps not-so-immodestly known as the "Greatest
Amateur Racing Event in the World." Each year, children from all

*David Fyne edges out Richard Cross by 1/10th second. Bryan Park Hill.
Lakeside, 1962.*

Sara Carpenter, competitor, Soap Box Derby at RIR, 2010.

over the globe descend on Akron, Ohio for the World Championships. But to get there, they have to win in their hometown first.

Richmond's soap box derby has been around since at least the '50s. Back then, the races took place over on Lakeside Avenue, down Bryan Park Hill. In the '80s, our derby boosters moved the race downtown, first to the mammoth hill on Canal, then Byrd, and then 2nd and 10th Streets.

Throughout its run – from the glory days of the '60s to the halcyon days of today – the soap box derby has been about craft, perseverance, and competition. According to an old brochure, the ingredients for success are a "look of cool determination," "steady hands," and in the background, of course, a "willing

Bob McDaniel, Jimmy Valentine - age 12, and Garland Gentry on scales at Soap Box Derby, 1955.

22

parent." To which I should add, an uncle, or troop leader, or for the kids at the Patrick Henry House who compete each year, a caring, community volunteer. The derby is nearly incongruous in these days of virtual action, animated, video sports. It might take a hundred hours of bruised thumbs to assemble a racing shell, all for the thrill of a 30-second race. But as I've learned from racers past and present, from the happy, wistful but determined looks in their eyes, the derby is about much more than can be packaged into a video game.

As Tennyson might say, the derby is not now what it once was, but it abides. And for a few hours on a Saturday in June, over by Gate 6 of the Richmond International Raceway, it will be recalled to life through the joyful noise of racers, and caregivers, and hopefully, our community at large. The event is free, the hill is wide, the steering is tight, and, as they say, the memories are priceless.

National Soap Box Derby Competition. Akron, Ohio, 1958.

New York Giants and Cleveland play at Mooers Field, 1946.

Our Fields of Dreams

Baseball in Richmond is a reflection of the city itself – old, abiding and brimming with stories, some nearly forgotten, others as familiar as yesterday's box score. Our oldest baseball stadium dates back to 1875 and was located within the fairgrounds at what is now Monroe Park. Since then, stadiums have come and gone, but their legacies persist.

Our most storied stadium was located on Mayo Island. First built in 1890 for a hometown team named the Richmonds, the stadium was replaced in 1920 with a modern facility known as Island Park. In 1926, the facility was renamed Tate Field in honor of one of the city's earliest baseball heroes, Pop Tate. The facility boasted a commanding view of the burgeoning Richmond skyline, as well as a roaring river

Tate Field, circa 1935.

The Diamond, circa 1985.

just beyond the left field fence. Alas, irreparable damage from a fire forced the demise of baseball on Mayo Island, for good, in 1941.

Broad Street also hosted its share of ballparks. The first was built at the intersection of Broad and Allen in 1896 with an enormous field that measured 560 feet to centerfield. Perhaps the most famous game ever played in Richmond took place at this field on October 10, 1911, before a bustling crowd of 9,000. The game pitted the Major League All-Stars, featuring Ty Cobb, against the Philadelphia Athletics, who went on to the World Series just a few weeks later. A newer Broad Street ballpark was built at the intersection of Broad and Addison in 1913 to host the Richmond Colts (a team that had four incarnations over time, first in 1894, then 1906, again in 1912, and last in 1918).

We have had our share of modern-era stadiums too. The first

of these was known as Mooers Field and was built in 1942 along Roseneath Avenue. The second was known as Parker Field and was built in 1954 along the 3000 block of North Boulevard. Parker Field opened on April 8, 1954, with an exhibition game between the Virginians and New York Yankees. And the last, but surely not the least, of our modern-era stadiums was built 25 years ago. Known then and now as the Diamond, the stadium was named in honor of the cooperation among the city, counties, fans, and team that brought it to fruition. Who knows, if we ever reprise this spirit of cooperation, maybe we'll be able to add a new stadium to the list. After all, our future is a reflection of our past.

Go Squirrels!

Parker Field, circa 1960.

King Arthur

Arthur Ashe was a tennis legend whose legacy extends far beyond the tennis court. And in the years since his untimely passing in 1993, we have only just begun to realize the full measure of our loss.

Ashe was born in Richmond in 1943. He learned to play tennis on the courts of Brook Field, a blacks-only recreational area where his father worked. When Ashe was six, his mother passed away. In this same pivotal period, Ashe met Ronald Charity, a student and tennis sensation at Virginia Union University. Charity coached Ashe for three years before turning the reins over to the great Dr. Walter Johnson of Lynchburg. Johnson was both a practicing medical doctor and a tennis enthusiast who served as coach, counselor, catalyst, and mentor to emerging stars like Ashe and Althea Gibson, who went on to win the French Open in 1956, as well as both the U.S. Open and Wimbledon in consecutive years 1957 and 1958. Under Johnson's watch, Ashe matriculated from schools in Richmond to St. Louis to Los Angeles and, then at last, to center court.

In a professional career marked by firsts at nearly every turn, Ashe's accomplishments defy simple listing. But the highlights

Arthur Ashe, Jr. and his father, Arthur Ashe, Sr. Fidelity Bankers Indoor Tournament at the Arena in Richmond, Va., May 3, 1968. Bill Lane Photo.

Arthur Ashe in a school room.

surely include his grand slam singles titles at the U.S. Open in 1968, the Australian Open in 1970, and Wimbledon in 1975 against a heavily-favored Jimmy Connors. By the time he retired in 1980, Ashe had chalked up a singularly impressive 818 wins and 51 titles.

Ashe's retirement from tennis was by no means one of choice. In 1979, he suffered a heart attack and was forced to undergo quadruple bypass surgery. Just four years later, in the midst of a second bypass operation, Ashe received a tainted blood transfusion from which he contracted HIV/AIDS.

But flagging health would not keep Ashe from taking on repeated and Herculean challenges off the court. Amidst many causes, Ashe tackled Apartheid, urban health care, human rights in Haiti, and HIV/AIDS. He received the Presidential Medal of Freedom in 1993. And he authored nine books, including his memoir and a three-volume treatise on the history of Black Americans in sports.

Ashe departed this world with two dreams left unrealized. The first was to build a National African American Hall of Fame here in Richmond. And the second persists in the words of his memoir:

My potential is more than can be expressed within the

bounds of my race or ethnic identity. My humanity … gives the greatest flight to the full range of my possibilities. If I had one last wish, I would ask that all Americans could see themselves that way, past the barbed wire fences of race and color.

Arthur Ashe was a superstar. He was a man of immense character, a humanitarian, and historian. And he was home-grown. May the Richmond that survives him live up to his legacy and one day, perhaps, realize the two dreams that Ashe left behind.

Ashe with tennis mentor Walter Johnson, and two colleagues.

Festival of Olympia, Richmond Style

From ancient times to modern, the Olympics have persisted as a symbol of international unity, athletic marvel, and games free from the compromises of commerce. Richmond may seem a wee bit off the beaten path for Olympic spirit, but we have a long and growing list of athletes who have dominated the Olympic stage, and we were a hair away from hosting the U.S. Olympic Festival in the late 1990s.

Joe Fargis with Touch of Class. Olympic Gold Medalist, show jumping, at the Summer Games in Los Angeles. 1984.

We have more than a score of Olympians to celebrate. Dr. Harold Thompson Mann grew up swimming in the Ginter Park Community Pool, became the first human being to swim the 100-meter backstroke in less than a minute, and won gold at the 1964 games in Tokyo. Joe Fargis and Conrad Homfeld rode stallions to individual gold and silver finishes, as well as team gold, at the 1984 games in Los Angeles. And Jon Lugbill, the guiding force of the Richmond Sports Backers, competed at the 1992 games in Barcelona, reinforcing his legacy as one of the most dominant whitewater paddlers in history.

To list is to miss, and surely others deserve mention – the fencer who trained at the downtown YMCA; the first baseman who learned his craft at J.R. Tucker High School; the Greco-Roman wrestler from

◀ *Whitney Hedgepeth, Olympic Medalist (1 gold, 2 silver) for swimming. Atlanta Games, 1996.*

33

Dr. Harold Thompson Mann, Gold Medalist - 100 Meter Backstroke. Olympic Games in Tokyo, 1964.

Highland Springs; Reid Priddy, who won a gold medal in men's volleyball at the 2008 Beijing Olympics; and Whitney Hedgepeth, who swam her way to three medals – two silver and one gold – at the 1996 games in Atlanta.

In 1994, Richmond vied to host the U.S. Olympic Festival, which ran for two decades as an off-year event to showcase Olympic-caliber athletes in training for the main event. We ended up in the final field of five cities and were considered a shoo-in to host the event in 1997, 1998, or 1999; a shoo-in, that is, until the organizers pulled the plug on the event altogether.

We certainly earned the right to host the festival, as our application was impressive in every respect. We had commitments of

support, funding, and infrastructure from every major corporate and community partner in the region, from the governor, to the mayor, to the county boards of supervisors,

Jon Lugbill, Olympian and 5-time world champion, for whitewater canoe slalom.

to corporations and churches of all sizes and denominations. We proposed a Metro Richmond Amateur Sports Complex in the area around the Diamond and Arthur Ashe Center, replete with a world class natatorium, ice rink, track and field oval, center court tennis stadium, tree-lined avenue of champions, and African American Sports Hall of Fame, which some will remember as one of Arthur Ashe's unfulfilled dreams. And we proposed sheer, unadulterated fun, with a mascot contest, youth sports initiative, and sporting events far and wide, from archery at UR to badminton at Collegiate, whitewater slalom at Belle Isle to judo at Manchester High School.

In our application for the Olympic Festival, we described Richmond as a "city with a history of making history." And we expressed a desire to be one of the East Coast's premier amateur sports centers.

We may have failed in our bid to host an Olympic festival. But we remain a city with a history of making history. And we excel in participatory sports. Festival or no festival, there's always someone challenging the limits of physical endurance, or athletic records of the past, right here in this Olympic village known as Richmond.

Bring it on.

Joe Fargis with Touch of Class.

35

The Bass Master

O! The gallant fisher's life, it is the best of any;
'Tis full of pleasure, void of strife and 'tis beloved by many.

~ Izaak Walton

Native Americans netted fish as they leapt from the falls of the James River long before any westerners found their way to Richmond. Captain John Smith recorded in his diary that when he and Christopher Newport's party explored their way up the James River to the "great craggy stones" that comprised the falls, his men only had to dip a skillet from the gunwale of the boat to catch fish. And, of course, for much of the last four centuries, the lure of the perfect catch has drawn many a Richmonder – young and old – to the river with rod and reel in hand.

Dr. Greg South, local angler extraordinaire. 1984.

In the 1950s, our Virginia Commission of Game and Inland Fisheries published a booklet that proclaimed "[a] state without fishlife and all that goes with it would be a sad place indeed." And in more recent years, local artist, writer, fisherman, and city enthusiast John Bryan published a book, *Urban Bassing in Richmond*, in which he offered fishing salvation to anyone with ten minutes, a 2-piece rod, a pocket tackle kit, a pack of baby wipes for slimy hands, tissues, rain gear, and a watch to keep on schedule.

Woo Daves displays catch in the Bass Masters Classic as Ray Scott looks on. August, 1988.

Woo Daves gets help with his crown from Dallas Hodges. August, 1990.

Our river is home to all manner of fish life, from sturgeon to shad to the king of sport fish, the largemouth bass. Described in nearly human terms as "complex, temperamental and moody," bass are a delightfully difficult beast to chase, given their stamina, courage, unpredictability, and "just plain cussedness." Bass react differently to qualities of light, noise, color, and odor, so bass fisherman are left to their wits to chose the right lure, line, and flick of wrist.

Of all the fish, and fisherman, and tall tales that have sprung from our river, the one that made the biggest splash was the BASS Masters Classic. BASS stands for Bass Anglers Sportsman Society, and the Classic is like the Super Bowl of fishing, bringing together 40 or so of the most accomplished anglers in the world to fish like they've never fished before for three straight days. Amazingly, Richmond hosted the Classic for three consecutive years (1988-1990), a "first and only" in the history of the event.

The rules of the Classic are fairly simple. The winner is determined by the heaviest three-day weight total. And each competitor is limited to five fish per day. You might think that the Classic draws a selective crowd of die-hard fishing fans, but 'tis not so. In 1988, the 12,000-seat Richmond Coliseum was standing room only, and fire marshals had to turn back over 1,000 fans trying to get a first-hand look at the weigh-in on the final day of the competition.

We lay claim to the Classic not just for its time here, but also for one of its finest competitors. In 1984, a Richmond physician, Greg South, qualified to be one of the nation's elite 40 to compete in the Classic. Though a relative unknown among a field of all-stars, South bested all of the other anglers except one, Rick Clunn, who was recently named the best bass angler of all time. South competed in the Classic two more times – in Chattanooga in 1986, and again before a hometown crowd in Richmond in 1988. In his last event, he got off to a mediocre start and considered pulling in a few smaller fish just to appease the local fans during the weigh-in. As he reported later, being "yanked up and down by the whims of a fish is a lot like romance." But ever the true competitor, he went for broke on the last day, fishing for the big one rather than compromising. He ended up empty handed at the weigh-in. "'Tis better to have fished and lost," he reflected, "than never to have fished at all."

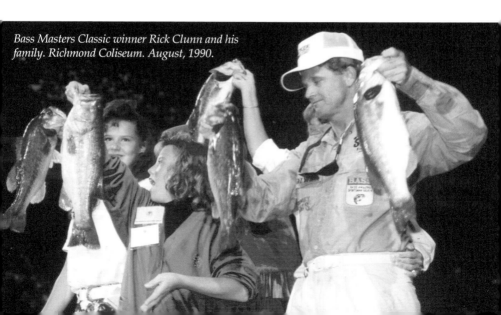

Bass Masters Classic winner Rick Clunn and his family. Richmond Coliseum. August, 1990.

The Old Lions
of the Richmond Marathon

I am told that there are different ways to write a story about a marathon. One is to tell it through the eyes and experience of a particular runner. Another is to tell it *en masse*. This one is a bit of both.

Garland Carlton, Philip Gibrall, Bill Smith, John Loughran, John Deeter and Tom Bednarz. 2010.

Our Richmond Marathon, which started in 1978, surely has inspired personal interest stories of immense weight, like the story of Dack Axselle, a boy suffering from spina bifida, who finished his first 5-mile race at the age of 8, his first half-marathon at the age of 9, and his first full marathon at the age of 10, all of them with leg braces and crutches.

The marathon has mass appeal too. Known for its 26.2 miles of smiles, our marathon has earned recognition as one of the best races in the country. We have unmatched scenery, from the old theatre district on Broad to the cobblestone Avenue of Monuments, the wonders of the James River, and the hidden haunts of the Northside. We have party zones, live music, wet washcloths, and junk food, not to mention "unofficial" beer and whiskey stops (or staggers). In 2009, more than 5,000 people ran the Richmond Marathon. If you

41

add in the 8k, half marathon and kids run, more than 15,000 people participated. And if you add in all of the cheering fans, well, you have the start of city-sized, city-wide party.

But this story is not so much about a particular runner or mass of running shoes. Rather, it is about six runners who by force or fluke of nature have eclipsed all others to become the Old Lions – the only runners to have completed each and every marathon since 1978: 33 races, 865 collective miles, and more than 45,000 accumulated minutes.

The Old Lions are Garland Carlton, John Deeter, Philip "Baltimore" Gibrall, John Loughran, Bill Smith, and Wertie Turner. They are joined by a few elite lion cubs, like "Tall Tom" Bednarz, who ran 100 marathons in 32 years, including 14 in Richmond.

For someone like me, aspiring to one day complete a marathon, the feats of the Old Lions are staggering. One Lion has run 105 marathons; another, 102. Still another has run two 100-milers and nine 50-milers.

1st Annual Richmond Newspapers Marathon
Richmond, Virginia - October 8, 1978

None of them set out to accomplish such feats when they signed up for the very first Richmond Marathon in 1978. For one, it was a dare; another, a simple desire to get in shape. All of them have a runner's regimen, not one of them alike. One ran two miles a day for 6,617 straight days. And all of them talk about runner's peace, the inability to run tense, and the repose and freedom that come with each passing mile.

For the Old Lions, running may be an inherently individual pursuit of mind and body, but it is also social and democratizing, and above all else, humanizing. As they described it to me, when you take the road, you don't care whether your running mates are bankers, lawyers, or bricklayers. You are all equal under the weight of the world treading on pavement, and your struggle is a common one. The Old Lions will be back on the pavement this November, and with any luck, you'll have a chance to follow them for a while. They are a special bunch, cut from a cloth of their own, and they deserve a collective roar for their effort. 43

First Cricket in America

Richmond can claim two unexpected superlatives in the league of "sports firsts" – the oldest recorded game of cricket in the New World and the earliest evidence of an organized cricket team in America. Lest there be any confusion, by "cricket"

Westover Plantation. Site for many early games of cricket.

I do not mean that little jumping bug of the family *Gryllidae*, but rather the game of bat and ball that spread with the British Empire and continues to inspire nearly religious fervor in over 100 countries around the world.

The oldest recorded game of cricket in the New World is credited to William Byrd II, founder of Richmond. In his *Secret Diaries*, Byrd offered sundry and delightful, if not occasionally absurd accounts of his whiles down at Westover on the James River. His (and the New World's) earliest reference to cricket dates back to an entry from May 6, 1709. But another entry provides unrivaled color on a day in the life of our city father, a member of the King's Council, a fellow of the Royal Society of Great Britain, author of the Westover Manuscripts, gentleman-farmer and cricketeer:

> March 28, 1710: I rose at 6 o'clock and read a chapter in Hebrew and some Greek in Anacreon. I ate milk for

breakfast and said my prayers. I danced my dance. About 10 o'clock Major Harrison, Hal Harrison, James Burwell and Mr. Doyley came to play at cricket. Isham Randolph, Mr. Doyley, and I played with them three for a crown. We won one game, they won two. Then we played at billiards till dinner, before which Colonel Ludwell came on his way to Mr. Harrison's. They all dined with us and I ate boiled pork. Soon after dinner the company went away and I took a nap. Then we walked to Mr. Harrison's, whom we found better. We played a game at cricket again. I took leave about 8 and returned home where I found Jenny better. I caused her to be cupped and then gave her pills. This was my birthday, on which I am 36 years old, and I bless God for granting me so many years. I wish I had spent them better.

Proof, perhaps, that a little idleness may nonetheless inspire greatness.

The earliest evidence of an organized cricket team in America is preserved right up the road at the Library of Virginia – the rules of the Richmond, Virginia Cricket Club, replete with the cost to join (1 dollar) and the penalty for missing practice (25 cents). An artifact, at best, but one that places Richmond out in front of Charleston, Boston, and New York City for the prize.

The rules of cricket may defy reason to an American audience more accustomed to the baseball diamond than an oval field of stumps, bails, bowlers, and batsmen, but the game persists, even here, in rec-league and elite teams harboring dreams of cricket greatness. And even if you don't know a sticky wicket when you see one, you'll still enjoy seeing a pitch or two. After all, as Lord Mancroft said, "cricket is a game, which the English, not being spiritual people, invented to give themselves some conception of eternity."

Tour de Richmond

Richmond is not quite Sports City, USA, but if you tally our horses, race cars, ball players, swimmers, and cricketeers, you might think twice. And if you throw in the second greatest cycling road race in the world, well, you might even start printing bumper stickers.

Most everyone knows about the Tour de France, the biggest and oldest cycling road race in the world. And most everyone knows the names of the great American road racers, Greg LeMond and Lance Armstrong. But too few recall that Richmond was part of a major race, perhaps the biggest in America, in which both LeMond and Armstrong competed and won.

The race debuted as the Tour de Trump in 1989 in honor of one of the few entrepreneurs audacious enough to try to rival the Tour de France. Richmond earned a stage on the first race and became so popular among the organizers, racers, and fans that it became the race headquarters in 1990. Even after Trump ceded to DuPont in 1991, Richmond persisted as the only city to participate

Start line, Tour De Trump, 1989.

◀ *Greg LeMond wins Tour, 1992.*

Cary Street, looking west. Photo by Tracey Reed Leverty.

in the event from its inception to untimely end in 1996.

Admittedly, the first race was considered a bit of an oddity in our fair city. But after a few years, it became one of the rites of spring, known not as the Tour De Trump or Tour DuPont, but simply and affectionately as The Tour.

The race drew a score of elite racing teams, with hundreds in each entourage, thousands of fans and millions of cycling fanatics watching the event from the comfort of their couches. It also brought some of the best sports writers and photographers from around the world to cover the event.

In 1996, Richmond earned both a stage and a circuit (cycling vernacular for a loop with hills). The circuit involved five laps through the heart of downtown and four climbs up Taylor's Hill on 23rd Street. It was so grueling that superstar Lance Armstrong was

Cary Street, looking east. Photo by Tracey Reed Leverty.

rendered nearly speechless. Pausing to talk to a reporter at the top of the hill, he could muster little more than "Phew!"

LeMond won the race in 1992; Armstrong in 1995 and 1996. For them, the other elite racers, and the solid line of spectators that formed miles outside of the city, Richmond conjured an atmosphere not unlike the cities of the *République Française*, with grand monuments, cobblestone streets, and old neighborhoods swarming with race enthusiasts.

Cycling road races may remain an oddity to some, but they draw from a common fabric. After all, everyone has ridden a bicycle at least once in their lives. And everyone feels some thrill (or thrilling fear) of speed. Perhaps that is why Richmond was able to capitalize not only on The Tour, but also its own Tour de Richmond, which served

as a warm-up for the big event and helped to profile the best of our local cyclists.

The Tour may be gone, but our cycling tradition abides. Way back in 1974, City Council went bike crazy and enacted a "bikeway" that ran from the Capitol to University of Richmond. We ought to restore it. And then, maybe, just maybe, we can start printing bumper stickers that read: "Let the races begin!"

The Original Nine: 1970 Virginia Slims Invitational

The "open" era of professional tennis began in 1968. But this did not mean equal pay for equal work. At the '68 Wimbledon, for example, the men's singles champion won $4,800; the women's singles champion, by comparison, only won $1,800. This inequality inspired nine professional women's players – dubbed the "Original 9" – to rebel and start their own professional women's tour. With the help of Joe

Rosie Casals, on the courts at the Westwood Club, 1970.

Cullman at Philip Morris, the tour became known as the Virginia Slims Invitational. And though history will reflect that the first Virginia Slims event took place in Houston, the actual tournament series kicked off right here in Richmond at the Westwood Racquet Club.

The appearance of the Original 9 in Richmond surely raised some eyebrows within the tennis establishment. But as the dean of Richmond sports writing, Jennings Culley, reflected:

> The tennis world's version of the women's lib has come to town and if you can forget the politics of the game, you'll find the young rebels are a delightful bunch of gals who – as the punsters say – have found tennis a game of love, not just a racquet.

Billie Jean King, on the courts at the Westwood Club, 1970.

Margaret Court receives award from Virginia Governor Linwood Holton, 1970.

Richmonders apparently took Culley's cue, because the event was standing room only. On opening night, November 5, 1970, more than a thousand people gathered to see Darlene Hard take on Denise Carter. Hard was known as the "last of the amateurs," earning little more than travel money for her wins at the French Open in 1960 and the U.S. Open in 1960 and 1961.

Even more people packed in for the finals, featuring the continuation of a great, running rivalry between Billie Jean King

54   *Virginia Wade, tennis clinic at the Westwood Club, 1972.*

and Nancy Richey. At the time, King was a three-time Wimbledon champion ranked third in the world. Richey was a two-time Grand Slam winner ranked second in the world. But on November 9, 1970, King was the better of the two, winning 6-3, 6-3 for a title purse of $2,400. Later in the day, King took the court again in the doubles finale, winning

with partner, Rosemary Casals, for a title purse of $400.

On the same day as King's victories in Richmond, the USLTA sought to ban the Original Nine, along with other contract professionals (including Rod Laver and Arthur Ashe) from all future tour events. But the bid failed, and the women finally got their due. For their efforts, the Virginia Slims' slogan was prophetic: "You've come a long way, baby!"

Westwood went on to host Virginia Slims events in 1972 and 1973 and continues to be a premier tennis club today. With our mark on women's tennis history, our claim to Arthur Ashe and a vibrant tennis scene with more than 27,500 active players, it is no wonder that Richmond is one of the best tennis towns in America.

Ray Dandridge

When the saints come marching in, let's hope they blow their horns extra loud for Ray Dandridge, a baseball superstar who almost didn't get his due. Ray was born in Richmond in 1913, attended what was then known as George Mason High School in Church Hill, and played for a number of Richmond amateur teams, including the Violets, All-Stars, and Grays, before turning pro.

As the story goes, Ray learned to play baseball in the cornfields around Church Hill. He and his friends would rake up a field, find a tree limb for a bat and engineer a makeshift ball out of twine and tape.

Ray's build was not classically athletic. Short, stocky and a wee bit bowlegged, he was known by his friends as "Squat." But with unparalleled defensive hands, "a train stood a better chance of going through his legs than a baseball." Ray was also a wildly consistent contact hitter, with a lifetime batting average well over .300.

Ray debuted with the Detroit Stars in 1933. After a few years in the American Negro Leagues, he migrated down to Mexico, where he played for almost a decade. When Jackie Robinson broke the color barrier in 1947, Ray returned to America to play minor league ball. At the age of 36, he was named Rookie of the Year for a Giants farm team

Ray Dandridge, 3B, Newark Eagles, 1942.

in Minneapolis. And at the age of 37, he was named league MVP. Around this same time, he roomed and played with an up-and-coming Willie Mays. But despite his many accomplishments, Ray was never called up to the major leagues. Maybe he was too old. Or maybe he couldn't beat the racial quotas of the day. Whatever the reason, it proved to be Ray's lament. As he reflected later, he just wanted to get his foot in the door, step in for one at-bat, or just have a cup of coffee.

Ray retired from baseball at the age of 41 without fanfare or horns.

He moved on. And then, at long last, he got his due. In 1987, Ray Dandridge was inducted into the Baseball Hall of Fame. "Thanks for letting me smell the roses," he said in his acceptance speech. "But what took you so long?"

Ray Dandridge passed away in 1994, leaving behind a legacy as one of the best third basemen

Ray Dandridge with Luke Easter, Cleveland Indian's first baseman. Mooers Field, 1950.

in baseball history. People said that he could field like Brooks Robinson and hit like George Kell. But his story is obscured by the shadows of a segregated game.

These days, it's hard to find a cornfield in Richmond. But you can find plenty of kids pulling down tree limbs for bats and making balls out of crumpled cardboard and tape. For them, and for Ray, let's all blow some horns.

Dandridge was inducted into the Baseball Hall of Fame in 1987.

Trophy room in his Palm Bay home. Dandridge is holding a trophy that commemorates a batting record for hits in 32 consecutive games, 1945.

More Than a Day at the Races

Richmond boasts two venerated racing traditions, one alive and well, the other just a shadow of the past. The first is the Strawberry Hill Races, built on a continuous legacy that dates back to 1895. The second is the Camptown Races, built on an equally old but episodic legacy that was renewed at Meadow

Camptown Races, Meadow Farm, circa 1955.

Farm, birthplace to the great stallion, Secretariat. And for horse enthusiasts, both remain far more than just a day at the races.

The Strawberry Hill Races originated with the Deep Run Hunt Club, which was chartered in 1887. Deep Run hosted its first steeplechase race in November 1895, and gave out its first Challenge Cup in May 1896. Back then, the races took place by University of Richmond near the intersection of River and Ridge Roads. In the 1920s, the races moved to Curles Neck Farm, just down river in Varina. Then, in 1947, the races moved to Strawberry Hill as part of the Atlantic Rural Exposition (a precursor to the State Fair). By mid-century, the races were as big a deal as any among the *haut monde* of Richmond. They were broadcast on WRVA and accompanied by all manner of special events, including a formal racing ball during which the men were required to wear "evening pink" – in effect, outdressing

President's Cup Carriage Trophy Winner, Vicky Carlisle, 2005.

their dates. The Strawberry Hill Races continue to this day at Colonial Downs, and draw so many spectators and celebrants that it is sometimes difficult to get a full view of the track itself, or the horses thundering through wings and over fences.

The Camptown Races drew from a tradition of flat country racing that originated in Ashland in the 1880s, back when the town was a summer resort equipped with a race track, jockey club, and betting salon. Country racing continued through the early 1900s at Bullfield, birthplace to the great antebellum race horse, Planet. Then, after a 50-year hiatus, the races were revived at Meadow Farm, birthplace to the more modern phenom, Secretariat. In 1960, the races moved to Manheim Farm to

better support the throngs of fans – up to 35,00 strong – that would come out for the event every spring. The Camptown revival inspired flat country races in Varina and Goochland, as well. Together, this country circuit became known as the "Little Triple Crown."

62

The Camptown Races continued through 1976. They were reprised for a brief run in the '80s but now are just a Richmond memory. Lest they fade for good, I wistfully offer two choice artifacts from the past. During the first running of the races in 1953, a Miss Nancy Jones "reined" supreme, winning both the "Ladies Race" and the elite "Hunters Race" on a chestnut mare named Symphonic. But those first races were not all speed and grace. They also featured a mule race won by a donkey named Kit. The newspaper reported Kit's run as a "start and stop affair, with a lot of weaving thrown in for good measure."

So, next time you find yourself track-side at Colonial Downs or side-tracked at the betting parlor, pray remember the steeplechasers that earned their legacy among the sport of kings, and the donkeys that, at least for a day, proved the old proverb that it is better to be the head of an ass than the tail of a horse.

Marshie Davis' Tailgate, Strawberry Hill Races.

Sue Clements and Bobby Allison at an appreciation event. May, 2008.

Southside Speedway:
The Toughest Short Track in the South

Motorsports draw hundreds of thousands of people to Richmond each year, honoring a tradition of automobile racing that dates back to the first half of the twentieth century. The city's premier racing venue, Richmond International Raceway, started as a dirt track in 1946 and hosted its first NASCAR Grand National in 1953. And though RIR is now synonymous with NASCAR, the early roots of stock car racing in our city actually trace back to both sides of the river.

Southside Speedway grew out of the old Royall Speedway, a quarter-mile dirt track that competed against other quarter-milers, like Mooers Field, through the late '40s and '50s. In 1958, Royall got out of the racing business and sold the track to J. M. Wilkinson, who quickly converted it into a third-mile, semi-banked, asphalt oval. The speedway

Start line. Car #11 was driven by Ray Hendrick, 1965.

Jimmie Walker, flagman.

hosted its first NASCAR Grand National race in 1961, beginning a series that would continue through the early '60s.

In the first year of the race, moonshiner and NASCAR Hall-of-Famer Junior Johnson took the prize. A year later, Jimmy Pardue rallied for a late win against NASCAR legend, Rex White, pocketing $550 for his Grand National victory. And in the third year, "Gentleman Ned" Jarrett traded leads with "The King" Richard Petty four times before Jarrett's Ford beat out Petty's Plymouth, snapping a seven-race win streak for the Plymouth team.

Over the decades, the Southside oval celebrated or subdued many of the greatest racers in the sport, earning a reputation as the "toughest short track in the south." And to this day, it continues a proud racing tradition with divisions for all manner of racing craft, from grand stock cars to modified, street, late model and U-cars (meaning cars that "you can afford to race"). It is also a family affair, home to three-generation racing families like the Hendricks (Ray, Roy and Brandon) and Hairfields (Ted, Bugs and Chris). Even some of NASCAR's most promising young stars, like Denny Hamlin, got their start at the speedway. In recent years, Denny has returned to the track with Kyle Busch, Tony Stewart, Elliott Sadler and other racing friends for a charity showdown, bringing well-earned attention to the venerable old track, not to mention raising awareness and funding for children with debilitating illnesses.

Southside Speedway may not be the biggest motorsports attraction in the city, but it has pedigree. And if you want to see racing like it used to be, then Southside Speedway is the place to go.

J. M. Wilkinson, Founder of Southside Speedway with his daughter, Sue Clements.

Denny Hamlin and Sue Clements, 2009.

Southside Speedway, 1973.

JOHNNY NEWMAN
1983-1986

Johnny Newman

Back in fifth grade gym class, in a basketball game with just seconds left on the shot clock, a point down, Johnny Newman drained a shot from half-court that won the game. The shot gave Johnny the confidence to believe that he could be good, very good, maybe even the best. From that moment forward, Johnny dedicated himself to out-working his competition.

Still just a scrawny kid from the country when he entered the University of Richmond in 1983, Johnny quickly distinguished himself with hard work on and off the court. In 1984, Johnny led the Spiders to their first-ever NCAA appearance, upsetting a fifth-seeded Auburn team that featured future NBA stars, Charles Barkley and Chuck Person. Two years later, the Spiders returned to the NCAA tourney, giving Johnny yet another chance to shine on the biggest stage of college basketball.

By the time he finished school, Johnny was Richmond's all-time leading scorer with 2,383 points. The scouts couldn't help but take notice of the points, percentages, or Johnny's work ethic. He was selected in the second round of the NBA draft in 1986, joining the Cleveland Cavaliers as the 29th overall pick. From there, Johnny

Banner recognizing Newman that hangs in the Robins Center, University of Richmond.

John Newman shoots over Auburn legend Charles Barkley (34) in the First Round of the 1984 NCAA Tournament (March 15, 1984) in Charlotte, NC. Newman scored a game-high 26 points to lead the Spiders to a stunning 72-71 triumph over Auburn in the first of Richmond's long list of noteworthy NCAA triumphs.

played 16 strong seasons around the NBA, holding his own against legends like Magic Johnson, Michael Jordan, and Larry Byrd. Among his favorite moments as a pro ball player, Johnny scored 35 points against the Celtics in his first playoff appearance. He went on to amass a total of 12,740 points in his NBA career.

These days, you will find Johnny at the helm of a successful Richmond-based property management company. But work does not stand in the way of an immense amount of time that he devotes to coaching, mentoring, and motivating kids all around the city and beyond. Johnny is proud to say that he makes kids smile every day.

He told me about an experience he had down in Charlotte, speaking to a group of troubled kids about the importance of getting on track and doing the right thing. A few of them tried to disrupt the talk but Johnny stuck to it, staying twice as long just to make sure the message got through. A year later, back in Charlotte, he was approached by some kids in a parking lot. They told him that they'd been in his class that day, had since graduated and were working, and wanted to thank him for caring enough to stick with them.

Johnny may be retired from pro ball, but he is not far from the game. He still sneaks in some court time at the Downtown Y every now and again. And he harbors dreams of returning to basketball as a coach. You can bet that Johnny would be the first to discover that next scrawny superstar from the country. And when the day comes for Johnny to coach, basketball will be better for it. After all, no one works harder, or with more heart, that Johnny Newman.

(L-R) Senior tri-captains Greg Beckwith (10), John Davis (32) and John Newman (20) raise the Richmond Times-Dispatch Championship Trophy after defeating Virginia, 58-46 in the title game Dec. 21, 1985. Newman was named Tournament MVP while Beckwith was named to the All-Tournament Team.

Newman is active in community support programs, as shown here with a Rotary check presentation associated with the Richmond Police Athletic League.

Virginia Boat Club

In 1876, a group of sandlot ballplayers bought a six-oared rowing shell and started the first rowing club in the city. In 1888, the club built a boathouse on Mayo Island and hosted its first regatta, drawing teams from as far away as Baltimore and Boston. In 1894, the Virginia General Assembly passed a law "to promote the healthful and manly exercise of rowing" through incorporation of the Virginia Boat Club. And over its proud history, the club distinguished itself, and our fair city, with rowing feats of the highest order.

Cups and trophies decked the walls of the old boathouse, reminders of storied wins like the Fredericksburg Cup in 1879; the French Cup in 1880, 1885 and 1894; and an open regatta victory at the Patapsco Navy Yard in Baltimore in 1889. In 1915, the club hosted the biggest regatta of its history against the Analostan Boat Club of D.C. and won practically every race. Through the first half of the 20th century, our club was dominant at home and on the road. We brought home trophies from victories in Philadelphia and New Orleans, including the "Super Bowl" regatta in 1940.

To be fair, our club suffered its share of losses, too. In 1910, we were beaten so badly by a team in D.C., that 25 years later, some members quipped that our

Virginia Boat Club Regatta, circa 1930.

73

1910 boat still hadn't crossed the finish line. And then there was the story of old Alfred "Crabber" Gray, Jr., who caught hold of a crab while rowing and was thrown completely out of his boat.

By mid-century, our club was more than just a bunch of accomplished and occasionally tall-tale-telling oarsmen; it was "high society." At its peak, the club boasted more than 500 members, a boathouse with vessels of every capacity, handball courts, a swimming pool, gymnasium, and of course, one of the prettiest views of the river in all of Richmond. Back in the day, club members honored a winter tradition of cutting holes in the ice and then jumping from roof to river amidst a bravado that if not healthful was surely manly.

But this is not to say that the club existed without dint of disaster. On Christmas Day 1929, the boathouse burned to the ground. Just over a decade later, it came within a few charred boards of burning down again in the fire that doomed its neighbor, Tate Field. In 1969, Hurricane Camille wrought her fury on Richmond, leaving up to five feet of standing water in the second floor of the boathouse. And in 1972, Hurricane Agnes drowned the old Mayo Island building for good. A few months after Agnes, the club was auctioned off to a local restaurateur for $22,000. Before he even had a chance to reopen the building, it was gutted by fire in 1974.

In the 1980s, a group of rowing enthusiasts revived the sport and introduced a whole new generation of Richmonders to rowing on the river. Like the sandlot ballplayers of old, they started with a boat and a dream. And like our crews from a century ago, they have earned distinction in regattas up and down the East Coast, not to mention our own Head of the James Regatta.

So whether you are a rank beginner, a recreational rower or a competitive racer, come on down to the river. The new Virginia Boat Club has a few oars waiting for you.

Regatta competition, at 14ᵗʰ Street Bridge.

Richmond "Pro" Football

"Ah, distinctly I remember it was in the bleak December…" and the dog days of winter held both baseball and football fans captive. Spring training seemed interminably distant. The stars were still aligning over that celestial event in the NFL calendar known simply and affectionately as the Super Bowl. And in Richmond, dear Richmond, that major market without a major franchise, boys in tattered jerseys huddled over frozen ground in pick-up games that may not have meant much to the outside world, but nonetheless had the potential to change the course of human events, at least for one reckless, rollicking, Hail Mary play.

These days, to find professional football in Richmond, you have to look indoors. In 2010, two professional teams debuted in our midst. The Raiders, of the AIFA League, stormed the Coliseum against competitors from places like Reading, Fayetteville and Baltimore. And the Revolution, of the IFL League, defended the Arthur Ashe Center against foes from Chicago, Rochester and Green Bay. Both teams gave our boys of winter a little razzle-dazzle to take back to their frozen sandlots. And both gave us hints of our storied football past.

"Pro" football in our fair city actually dates back to the 1930s, when our Richmond Rebels were part of the fabled Dixie Pro Football League, sometimes called the third of the three majors. Dixie Pro was

Richmond Raiders All-Star Game, Richmond Coliseum, January, 2010.

Richmond Roadrunners coach J. D. Roberts with flanker, Jon Robinson, 1969.

formed in 1936, suspended during World War II, and then revived in 1946. Back then, our Rebels were affiliated with the burnished Steelers of Pittsburgh.

In 1947, the Rebels defected to the American Football League. A few years later, we had the tenacity to take on the Chicago Bears in an exhibition game. The Bears outscored us 47-14, but if you paused to read the postmortem in our local paper, the game was closer than it looked.

The next two decades marked a topsy-turvy time in "pro" football. Richmond's AFL team disbanded in the early 1950s, then reorganized a decade later as part of the Atlantic Coast Pro Football League.

Richmond Roadrunners coach J. D. Roberts with starting quarterback, Ronnie South, 1969.

During the 1965-66 season, we defected to the Continental Football League. But by 1968, we were back in the Atlantic Coast League as the Richmond Roadrunners, a minor league farm team for the marching Saints of New Orleans.

Eventually, the NFL dropped its farm system, and minor league professional affiliates like the Roadrunners faded from the scene. But even without a team, Richmond continued to be a pro football destination. On August 7, 1968, the New York Jets played their season opener against Joe Namath and the Boston Patriots right here at City Stadium. Proceeds from the game were donated to a summer camp for diabetic children. In 1973, Richmond vied for an NFL expansion team and even partnered with the surrounding counties to explore the

feasibility of housing such a franchise. And in 1985, we almost landed a Canadian Football League team. But alas, none of our prospects panned out.

Richmond Roadrunners owner Bill Templeton with New Orleans Saints owner John Mecom, Jr. and others. City Stadium, 1968.

Beyond indoor football, Richmond remains a major market without a major franchise. But don't tell the boys in tattered jerseys playing their guts out in frozen sandlots all over the city. For them, it just doesn't matter. Football is a game to be played.

New York Jets coach Weeb Ewbank with star running back Matt Snell and rookie Lee White before an Exhibition game between the Jets and the Boston Patriots. City Stadium, 1968.

Best Road Race in the Southeast: Ukrops Monument Avenue 10k

I have only been seized with the inspiration to run – "to go quickly" as Noah Webster would say – twice. The first time was on the top of Old Rag Mountain. And the second was at the finishing stretch for the Monument Avenue 10k.

I love the woods. I love the tonic of the woods, the hush, the hum, the crunch of leaves underfoot. I love that first rush of adrenaline when you hit a trailhead, those first thousand feet of amazement when you leave your material life behind and enter a more primordial one. And more than anything else, I love woods that rise with the hills and cede with the summits, giving way to great craggy stones and wide-open vistas that literally expose the forest from the trees.

On an occasional morning, I will rise before the dawn and let the coffee steam my windows as I streak west into the hills. But the story I am about to tell is an even more singular one. I remember hitting the trail head for Old Rag around 6:15 a.m., so giddy with anticipation that I left all my goodies, including my water, in the car. I scrambled to the top. I paused. I chose the more meandering back way down. And I was so happily lost

Starting line, Ukrop's 10K, 2010.   81

in the delights of my trail dreams that I nearly walked smack-dab into a bear. Seriously. Now I cannot fairly attest to the size or demeanor of the bear, for I am no judge of such things. Suffice it to say that in my mind's eye, the bear was a huge, raving beast. And in that moment – that first reflexive "what do you do" moment – I had only two thoughts, neither of them sanctioned by the Boy Scouts of America: climb a tree or run. I chose the latter. That poor old bear never even saw me coming. He just felt the wind rush through his hair as I rocketed down the mountain, running faster than I ever had, or would, in my life. I ran so fast that the leaves didn't even crunch underfoot. I ran like a man possessed, wild-eyed, racing from the jaws of a bear still idling along the path munching berries and dreaming of his long winter's rest. You will not find this image in the definition of "run" in old Noah Webster's dictionary, but for me, the two are inextricably linked.

Last year, I ran the Monument Avenue 10k with my big brother. He is a runner's runner – lithe and light with lungs like bellows. If you saw us at the starting gate, you would have said that he cut through the air like a knife. If you were charitable, you would have said that I

tumbled forward, apparently saved from falling by the sheer weight of the air around me. But when you are surrounded by 37,000 runners, and at least an equal number of cheering fans, even the worst runner gets a lift.

Race-side entertainer on Monument Avenue.

By the time we turned the corner on Lombardy and caught the first live band of the day, I was actually having fun. And after a few more miles of music, improbable costumes, spirit groups and revelers, I was happily lost in the delights of the race. Near the end, I was amazed to find myself just a step behind my brother. He looked like he was game for a little competition. So I nodded in ascent, closed my eyes, conjured up that big old bear, and ran like a man possessed.

Bob Dylan said you might find your inspiration in the songs of Woody Guthrie, the Grand Canyon, or the streets of Rome. For me, it lurks in the trail head at dawn and the Monument Avenue 10k. It may be only my experience, but "to go quickly," it helps to have a bear in your head.

Justin Verlander

You don't need me to tell you that Justin Verlander is a baseball superstar. His stats speak for themselves. In just his first five years in the major leagues, Justin has amassed a long list of superlatives: AL Rookie of the Year (2006); Major League All-Star (2007, 2009, 2010); AL Wins Leader (2009); AL Strikeouts Leader (2009). He has won at least 10 games in each and every season of his major league career, at least 15 in four of them. And in 2007, Justin threw his first big league no-hitter.

Justin Verlander with his father & coach, Richard Verlander, while playing Tuckahoe Little League baseball.

No, you don't need me to tell you that Justin is a superstar. But with some help from his dad, I might be able to explain how he became one.

Justin was born in Manakin-Sabot in 1983. He was a normal kid in a family that relished (and still relishes) normalcy. To his parents, Justin was just Justin, and he remains "just Justin" to this day. They raised him and his younger brother (a rising superstar, as well) to appreciate the qualities of hard work, and they loved and cared for their boys just as any good parents would. They did not dispense any magic potions; just good old-fashioned working class and family values.

Justin Verlander in his rookie year with the Detroit Tigers.

Justin and fiancée, Emily.

Justin started playing t-ball when he was six, and was in every respect a regular kid in a typical sandlot setting. The first signal of his talent came a few years later when he and his dad were skipping rocks in Deep Run Park. Justin's dad tried to throw a rock across the lake but couldn't do it. Then Justin tried. His rock sailed over the lake and beyond. His dad described it as a "pinch me" moment – one of many more to come – when he witnessed the sheer physical potential of his son's throwing arm.

I asked his dad what advice he'd give to other parents. He said to

Verlander family poses with the framed jersey retiring Verlander's number from Goochland High School.

enjoy the journey. It is not about the destination but the experience. If your kid likes to play ball, then let him play ball. If he's good at it, then enjoy his success. But don't get caught up in the next level. Let him play the best he can in whatever level he's in.

The Verlanders are living the dream, and they know it. But what makes them special is that they've been living and cherishing the dream since Justin was a little kid – long before he was a superstar or unveiled his superstar arm. Justin's dad described his excitement now as being no different than watching Justin play little league, or high school, or college baseball – the excitement of a father, any father, seeing his kid work hard and do well. And that, I think, is the key to the dream.

Richard Verlander (father), Ben Verlander (brother), Kathy Verlander (mother), Justin and his fiancée, Emily, on America Field in Detroit, Michigan during the World Series, 2006.

Placemat created to help celebrate the Goochland Chamber's Justin Verlander Day in 2007.

87

The Beautiful Game

Soccer is the world's most popular sport. The game, known to purists as association football, dates back to 1863 in the Old World and 1869 in the New. But it took Brazilian footballers like Pelé in the 1970s to popularize the sport in the United States, and even more recent footballers like Mia Hamm to democratize it among men and women.

In Richmond, Thomas Jefferson High School became the first and only local public school with a soccer team in 1964. A year later, employees from two German companies, homesick for the game, formed the Richmond Soccer League, which later became the Central Virginia Soccer Association, an adult soccer league that now boasts nearly 100 teams and over 8,000 registered players.

Richmond Kickers pro player Mike Burke and president of the board of directors, Rob Ukrop, conduct a clinic for the Boys & Girls Club and Police Athletic League at Richmond City Stadium. Photo by Willie Riefner.

By the early '70s, with help from the city's soccer patriarch, Dave Amsler, all of Richmond was abuzz with soccer. Amsler organized the first summer soccer league in 1972, with eight teams and 125 players, all high school age or older. By 1977, the league had grown to seven divisions covering all ages from 2-year old "mites" to full-sized adults. Around this time, Amsler also organized the first travel soccer team in

Richmond Kickers U12 Boys versus FC Richmond, at the Kickers state-of-the-art sports complex, Ukrop Park. May, 2010. Photo by Aukse Wirz.

89

the city, the Richmond Strikers. Still strong today, the Strikers host the annual Jefferson Cup, which is one of the country's premier soccer tournaments for boys and girls, drawing upwards of 30,000 visitors to the city, including hundreds of college coaches and recruiters. After NASCAR, the Jefferson Cup is the biggest sporting event in the city. A decade after starting the Strikers, Amsler organized another fine club, FC Richmond, which he still directs to this day.

"Pro" soccer entered the scene with the Richmond Kickers in 1993, then a member of the USISL and now USL-2. In '95, the Kickers won both the USISL Premier League Championship and the U.S. Open Cup, among the most cherished of soccer prizes. This big-time splash helped Richmond land the NCAA Division 1 men's soccer final four from '95 through '98, a run that earned the city national, if not international attention.

These days, soccer is more than a fever. It is an epidemic. A field

without soccer is a poor field indeed. With youth, school, college, adult, and advanced leagues, clubs and programs interspersed throughout our region, Richmond can lay claim to literally tens of thousands of soccer players. And they are more diverse in age, race, gender, and ethnicity than any other sport in town.

Soccer phenom, Rob Ukrop, has seen all of the glories of the game. A standout at Davidson College, Ukrop led the nation in scoring in 1992.

During the 1995 U.S. Open Cup, Ukrop was MVP of the championship game. And for a sustained professional career, Ukrop got to tangle with the best footballers in the world. But these days, his greatest joy is introducing new kids to the sport, and helping them develop the teamwork, discipline and hard work that will produce success both on and off the field.

Richmond Kickers midfielder Mike Burke hoists the USL Second Division trophy after the Kickers claimed their second title in the past four seasons, 2009. Photo by Brian Zimmerman.

For Ukrop, the inclusiveness of soccer as a sport for all ages, races, genders and ethnicities is proof that soccer is, as Pelé once said, "the beautiful game."

A full-house at Richmond City Stadium witnessed the Kickers pro team claim their second USL Second Division title. August 29, 2009. Photo by 2010 Brian Zimmerman.

Billy Fox knocks light heavyweight Artie Levine to the canvas in the third round at Madison Square Garden, 1947.

"Blackjack" Billy Fox

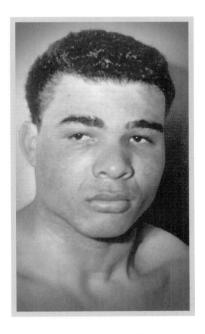

To end up with a nickname like "Blackjack," you need to show some hustle. For "Blackjack" Billy Fox, he found all the hustle he needed right here in Richmond.

As a transplant from Oklahoma growing up in Richmond, Fox hustled all manner of odd jobs. He delivered papers, shined shoes, set bowling pins, and helped tend to the family garden. He also got into his share of scrapes at school, distinguishing himself as a quiet but querulous kid.

At the age of 16, Fox quit high school and ran away from home. His worldly possessions at the time were a bicycle, a book on boxing, and a penny in his pocket. He rode from Richmond to Appomattox, sold his bike for bus fare and then wended his way north, first to D.C., then to New York, and finally to Philadelphia.

In South Philly, Fox worked days and boxed nights. Over the next few years, under the management of a shady mobster, Frank "Blinky" Palermo, Fox amassed a record of 36 consecutive knock-outs (occasionally hyperbolized as 49) and earned a shot at the world light heavyweight title. The bout took place at Madison Square Garden on February 28, 1947, and featured Fox against Gus Lesnevich in a barnburner brawl that went 10 rounds. Lesnevich knocked Fox down

93

Billy Fox works out in Summit, NJ, 1947.

for an eight-count in the tenth. Fox stumbled to his feet and tangled Lesnevich to the mat, but then the ref called the fight as a TKO for Lesnevich.

Down but not out, Fox took his 36 and 1 record back to the gate and won 7 straight in his bid for a rematch. Among his come-back bouts was one against Jake LaMotta on November 14, 1947, immortalized in Martin Scorsese's movie, *Raging Bull*. LaMotta, a bruiser from the Bronx, was the first boxer to beat Sugar Ray Robinson. But in his fight against Fox, LaMotta was more butterfly than bull, going down peremptorily in just four rounds. LaMotta initially blamed his poor showing on a spleen injury that he had suffered in training, but the rest of the world suspected that the fix was in. More than a decade later, LaMotta confessed to a Senate committee on organized crime that he threw the fight in exchange for a promise from the Mafia to give him a future shot at the title.

For his part, Fox earned a rematch against Lesnevich just a few months later but the bout was a bust. Fox was dropped twice and then knocked out less than two minutes into the first round. He continued to box afterwards, but the stain of the LaMotta affair changed the course of his life. In 1956, a reporter for *Sports Illustrated* found him "desolate, vagrant and despairing" on the streets of New York. By the time of the Senate hearings in 1960, Fox was believed to be a patient at a mental hospital in Long Island. After that, he simply faded away.

"Blackjack" Billy Fox was a mythical boxer with a career record of 48 wins (47 by KO), 9 losses and 1 draw. He had a hustle that took him to the top of his game, almost to the top of the world, and then down and out. By the end of his life, he was back to setting bowling pins, just like his early days in Richmond. A cautionary tale, perhaps, but one that has a source with a kid on a bicycle in our fair city, with nothing more to his name than a book on boxing and a penny in his pocket.

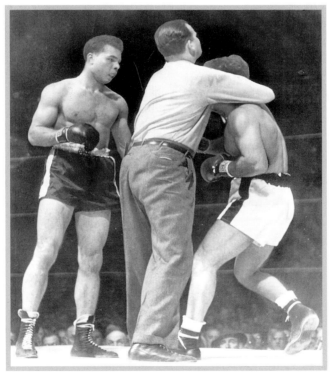

Referee Frank Fullam steps between Jake LaMotta and Billy Fox to stop their fight in the 4th round. November 14, 1947.

The Baseball Tradition

Few sounds permeate modern life more universally than the whish of a fastball, the crack of a bat or the expectant inhale of the teeming fans as their outfielder dashes past the warning track to reel in a high fly ball. And, surprisingly, few places are steeped in the lore of the old ball game more than Richmond.

Mayor Stirling King prepares to launch the local Piedmont League season. He is flanked by Ray Schalk, Newport News manager, and Richmond Colts manager Vinnie Smith. Mooers Field. April 26, 1949.

Our baseball roots date back to 1867, when our hometown favorites, the Richmond Pastimes, were scuttled 53 to 25 by an upstart Charlottesville team in the Championship of Virginia. Back then, players fielded balls with their caps or even barehanded. And the umpires wore top hats and ties to distinguish themselves before rowdy crowds rumored to bellow "shoot the hat" instead of "kill the ump" to signal their disfavor over a bad call.

Our first professional team, the Richmond Virginians, emerged in 1884, and again in 1917 and '54. Following them were the Colts in 1894, revived by popular demand at least four times in the following century. Then the Bluebirds, the Lawmakers, the Climbers, the Byrds (with a "y" that is) and, of course, the Braves. Our teams were storied. They checkered the sky with pennants. In 1895, we took one from

Richmond Flying Squirrels mascot, Nutzy.

the Roanoke Goats; in 1908, from the Danville Bugs. And again and again over the years, Richmond distinguished itself among baseball's elite.

Our players were larger-than-life, with ludicrous nicknames and seemingly impossible records. Our 1906 team featured "Bonehead" Bobby Wallace in the outfield and "Thousand Percent" Jack Quinn on the mound, earning his moniker after going 14-2-0 in 1908. We had "Barley" Kain, "Pop" Tate, "Hitch-em-up" Shaeffer and "Cocky" Magolis, a cross-eyed southpaw who set a record in 1919 for the number of runners he picked off at first. As his victims reported, "we could never tell which way he was looking."

And in the chiaroscuro of baseball's tortured past, we had the best of both black and white. Our first professional black team emerged in 1903 as the Reformer All-Stars, and they were so good as to integrate

an otherwise divided city. On April
28, 1903, they thwacked the New
York Cuban Giants 25 to 4 before an
exuberant mixed crowd at the old
Broad Street Park. Later, this same
inspired crowd would celebrate
a man with hands of velvet, Ray
Dandridge, as he rose from the

Richmond cornfields to become one of the greatest third basemen in
history, black or white.

Baseball is a tradition of teams and players and encyclopedic
accomplishments. It is also a tradition of parents and children, bleacher
seats on a Sunday afternoon, ballpark hotdogs loaded with yellow
mustard, the whish of a fastball and the crack of a bat. Baseball may no
longer be our undisputed national pastime, but it still tugs at the heart.
And when the anthem rolls and the first pitch comes in, you can bet that
the stands of the Diamond will be filled with families clasping hands and
pointing out expectantly into the field of glory. I hope to see you there!

Afterword

For a city steeped in history, sports are a lens through which
to view and try to understand our storied past. Sports may appear
frivolous in comparison to the lenses of struggle and conflict, but they
are no less redemptive, or unifying, or telling of the immense potential
of the human body and spirit. Think Arthur Ashe.

And sports, more than any other strand of our city's fabric, tap
into that great, harmonizing, equalizing, democratizing dream of every
man and woman – that on any given day, on any given field, or court,
or lane, or fairway, the impossible could happen. The hole-in-one, the
winning ace, the no-hitter, the walk-off home-run. The impossible has
happened. Think Ray Dandridge.

The sports stories of our city are incongruous (think cricket),
quirky (think quoits), and sometimes apocryphal, like the one about
Babe Ruth hitting a home run out of Tate Field into a coal car headed
for Baltimore – surely the longest home run in history if not for
similar claims made by the Atlanta Crackers, the Norfolk Tars, and
countless other teams and cities all across America.
We have enjoyed our share of head-
scratchers (think of
Sammy Snead's

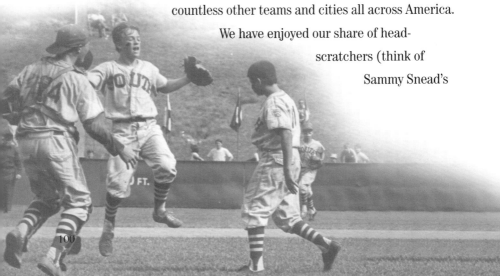

win with a borrowed putter) and tear-jerkers (think of Dack Axselle's marathon with leg braces and crutches). And we have almost lost a few that are terribly important, like the story about the Richmond Reformer All-Stars, a black professional team that on April 28, 1903, took on the Cuban Giants of New York at Broad Street Park before the biggest crowd of the season, and one that was equally mixed black and white. The Cuban Giants were the first black professional team in America and were considered to be the best in the land. But on this day of rarified air here in Richmond, our Reformer All-Stars shellacked them 25 to 4.

Alas, like any exploration of our fair city, the greatest risk is one of omission. This little book is not an encyclopedia. It hints at what makes the sports of our city so special, but it surely omits many stories worth telling. I wish I had room for a chapter on Willie Lanier, the football superstar from Maggie Walker High School who led the Chiefs to the Super Bowl and earned the nickname "Contact" through the sheer force of his head-first defensive play. And another on Barty Smith, the football superstar from Douglas Freeman High School who led the Spiders to the Southern Conference Title before taking a more national stage with the Packers.

More than anything, I wish I had room to tell the stories of the coaches (think Stretch Gardner and Maxie Robinson), the sports writers (think Jennings Culley), and above all else, the parents. Without them, the lens would be empty.

Richmond is a great sports town. We have much to celebrate. And even more to play. So go and do. The fields and fairways beckon.

Acknowledgements

This book features stories that aired on WCVE Public Radio as part of Brooks' *Rediscovering Richmond* series. They would not have materialized without the support of the Community Idea Stations, their family of supporters and listeners, or the principle of creative expression on which public radio is based.

The stories come from the people who lived them or took the time to record them. Some of the stories would never have found the printed page without the goodness of librarians at the Library of Virginia, Richmond Public Library, Valentine Richmond History Center and Virginia Historical Society. We owe deep gratitude to all of the people who took time to tell, share, and find.

The photographs come from archives all around the city, chief and best among them, the archives of the *Richmond Times-Dispatch*. If you do not subscribe to the paper, you should. The *RTD* is both news-maker and news-keeper. And though the former keeps the lights on, the latter is what sparks the inner-light. In the collections made available for this book, the *RTD* has given us all a hint of the treasures of our past – treasures that the *RTD* preserves not because it must but because it can.

We tip our helmets, yell "fore" and extend high-fives to the following individuals and organizations that helped us fill these pages:

"Tall Tom" Bednarz	Jayne Hushen	Greg South
Andrea Bedson	JoLynn Johnson	Shelly Sowers
John Bryan	Leeanne Ladin	Hank Stoneburner
Garland Carlton	Tracey Leverty	Wertie Turner
Sue Clements	John Loughran	Kate Tweedy
Richard Cross	Jon Lugbill	Rob Ukrop
Marshie Davis	John Mizelle	Richard Verlander
John Deeter	Johnny Newman	Black History Museum
JR Downey	Nutzy	Library of Virginia
Danny Finnegan	Gray Oliver	Richmond Public Library
David Fitzgerald	Jim Pankovits	Richmond Sports Backers
Margaret Galloway Ford	Mike Plant	Valentine Richmond History Center
Elizabeth & Michael Fraizer	Scott Schricker	Virginia Historical Society
Philip "Baltimore" Gibrall	Bill Smith	Westwood Club

And we bow to our children, who help to keep our sporting dreams alive.